PLUTO

A TRUE BOOK

by

Larry Dane Brimner

Children's Press®
A Division of Grolier Publishing

New York   London   Hong Kong   Sydney
Danbury, Connecticut

Clyde W. Tombaugh discovered Pluto in 1930.

Subject Consultant
Peter Goodwin
Science Department Chairman
Kent School, Kent, CT

Reading Consultant
Linda Cornwell
Learning Resource Consultant
Indiana Department
of Education

Author's note:
Special thanks to the staff
at the University of
Arizona's Lunar Planetary
Lab and San Diego's
Palomar Observatory for
answering questions and
confirming information.

Author's dedication:
For Meridian Elementary
School, where it all began

Visit Children's Press® on the
Internet at:
http://publishing.grolier.com

Library of Congress Cataloging-in-Publication Data

Brimner, Larry Dane.
    Pluto / by Larry Dane Brimner.
        p.   cm. — (A true book)
    Includes bibliographical references and index.
    Summary: Discusses the smallest, most distant, and most mysterious
planet in our solar system, its discovery, and its peculiar orbit.
    ISBN 0-516-21155-2 (lib.bdg.)   0-516-26499-0 (pbk.)
    1. Pluto (Planet)—Juvenile literature. [1. Pluto (Planet)] I. Title. II.
Series.
QB701.B75 1999
523.48'2—dc21   98-26740
                                                                                    CIP
                                                                                    AC

GROLIER
PUBLISHING

Contents

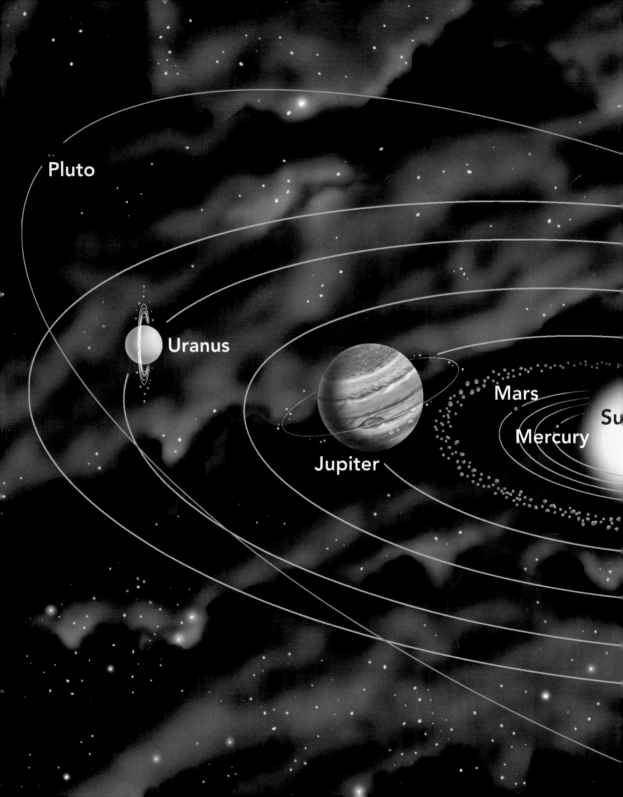

The Solar System

Venus

Moon

Earth

Asteroid Belt

Saturn

Neptune

Bigger and Bigger

Planets are large objects that travel, or orbit around the Sun. These planets, along with all the other objects that travel around the Sun, make up our solar system. Early astronomers thought that only six planets orbited the Sun. They believed Saturn was the

People have always been interested in looking at the night sky. But early telescopes were not strong enough to see deep into space.

most distant planet. Human eyes and early telescopes could not see any farther.

By the 1700s, telescopes were more powerful. They helped astronomers find a seventh planet, Uranus, in 1781. Could the solar system be even bigger? Many astronomers thought so. They continued to search. Finally, in 1846, they found Neptune.

Eight planets! The solar system was getting bigger and bigger. It wasn't until 1930 that an astronomer discovered the ninth and farthest planet

Pluto was the Roman god of the underworld.

from the Sun—Pluto. It was named Pluto, after the Roman god of the underworld—a good name for a planet so far off in space.

Planet X

Both Neptune and Pluto were found because astronomers were looking for a "missing planet." Many astronomers believed there was a giant planet somewhere beyond the seventh planet, Uranus. They called it Planet X.

Uranus (left) had a strange orbit that made scientists think there may be another planet beyond it.

Astronomers thought there must be another planet because of Uranus's strange orbit. They could figure out the orbits of most of the planets, but not the orbit of Uranus. Sometimes it sped up and sometimes it slowed down. It was difficult to know just where to look for Uranus.

Many astronomers thought Uranus's odd behavior was caused by Planet X's gravity. Gravity is the force that pulls objects toward a planet's center. It is the same force that makes an apple fall to the ground when it drops from a tree here on Earth. Scientists

Gravity can be seen on Earth when an apple falls to the ground.

thought that Planet X's gravity must be pulling on Uranus. So they began to look for the giant planet.

Then they found Neptune. But Neptune behaved oddly, too—just like Uranus. So some astronomers believed that they still had not found Planet X. American astronomer Percival Lowell (1855–1916) set up Arizona's Lowell Observatory to search for it.

In 1930, a young astronomer at the observatory spotted a dim point of light. News reports said young Clyde W. Tombaugh (1906–1997) had found Planet X. The farthest

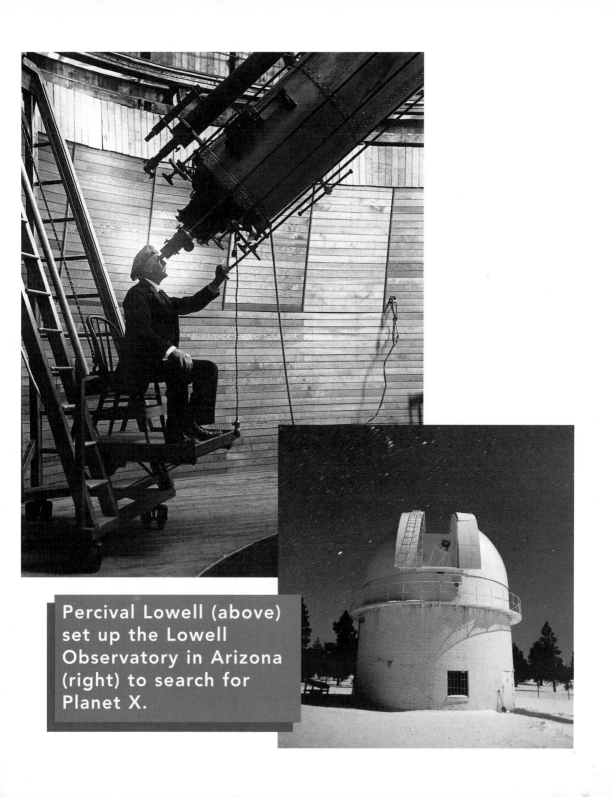

Percival Lowell (above) set up the Lowell Observatory in Arizona (right) to search for Planet X.

Clyde W. Tombaugh

planet in our solar system, Pluto is an average of 3.7 billion miles (5.9 billion kilometers) from the Sun.

New Planets

A drawing of the star 51 Pegasi and its planet

Is Earth the only planet that supports life? Is our solar system the only solar system? Since 1995, astronomers have found several new planets in other solar systems beyond our own. The first planet found outside our own solar system is orbiting a star called 51 Pegasi. This is a star like our Sun. At least two other solar systems have also been found. These solar systems may have planets that can support life. Perhaps some- day we will know for sure.

What We Know

Probes, or spacecraft, have told us a lot about our solar system. But no probe has ever flown close enough to Pluto to study it. Even the Hubble Space Telescope— a giant telescope orbiting in space—cannot get a clear picture of Pluto. This

18

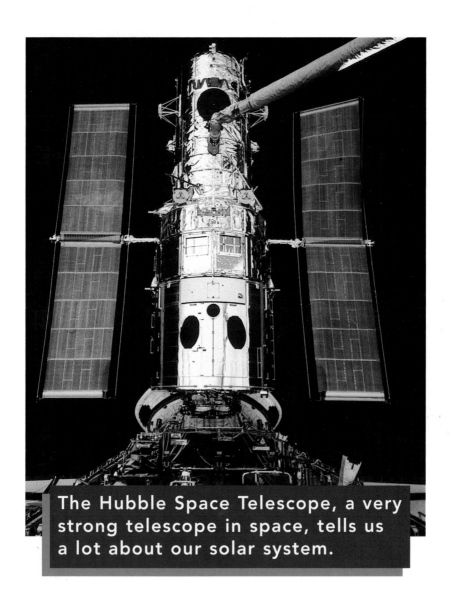

The Hubble Space Telescope, a very strong telescope in space, tells us a lot about our solar system.

planet is the solar system's biggest puzzle.

Pluto is even smaller than the Earth's Moon.

Astronomers have been able to learn a few things, however. Pluto is the smallest planet in our solar system. It is only 1,412 miles (2,272 km) across. This is smaller than our own Moon.

A planet's year is the time it takes for that planet to make one orbit around the Sun. It takes Earth one year—365 days—to make its journey. It takes Pluto 248 Earth-years to complete one orbit.

The paths of most planets around the Sun are elliptical, which means they are shaped like a stretched-out circle. But Pluto's orbit is more narrow and stretched out. Its unusual orbit sometimes puts Pluto nearer to the Sun than Neptune. Between February 1979, and February 1999, Neptune—not Pluto—was the most distant planet in the solar system.

Most planets have north and south poles that point almost straight up and down as they orbit the Sun. But two planets—Uranus and Pluto—are different. Their poles tilt to the

Pluto (above) has a long and narrow orbit.

side. Each of the planets rotates, or spins, on its axis as it orbits the Sun. An axis is an imaginary line between a planet's north and south poles. Earth spins once every 24 hours. So the length of Earth's day is 24 hours. Pluto rotates once about every 6.5 Earth-days.

Pluto is frozen and dark. Scientists think it is probably a mixture of rock and ice. Its surface temperatures are

Pluto and its moon rotate as they orbit the Sun.

between −378 to −396 degrees Fahrenheit (−228 to −238 degrees Celsius). It would not be a comfortable place to visit!

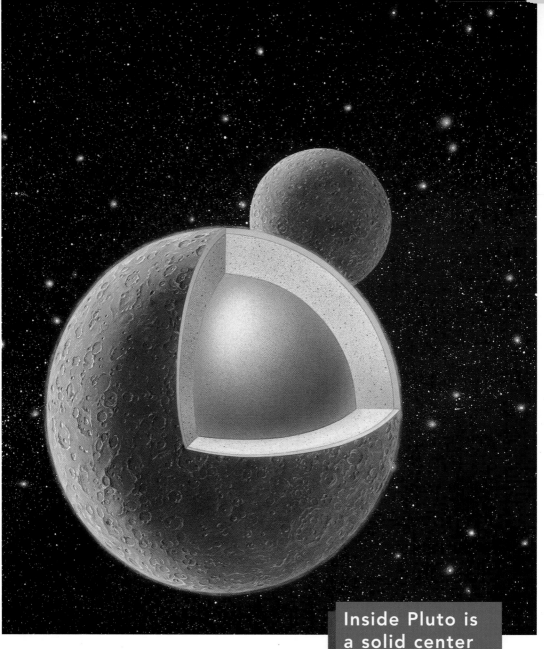

Inside Pluto is
a solid center
surrounded by
a thick layer of
rock and ice.

The gases that surround Pluto make up its atmosphere. Scientists believe that Pluto's atmosphere is mostly made up of the gas nitrogen, with smaller amounts of carbon monoxide and methane. Pluto's atmosphere may be in the form of gas only when the planet is closest to the Sun. Some scientists think its gases may freeze when Pluto moves away from the Sun.

Pluto's Moon

Pluto's moon Charon was discovered in 1978. It is a small moon, but it is still more than half the size of Pluto. Scientists think Charon's surface is covered with ice.

When scientists first found Pluto, they thought it was bigger than it really is. Pluto

This photograph of Pluto and Charon was taken by the Hubble Space Telescope.

and Charon are so far away that they looked like one object, not two. Today, some people even think of Pluto and Charon as two planets rather than a planet and a moon.

The Kuiper Belt

In the 1950s, astronomer Gerard Kuiper (1905–1973) had an idea. He believed there was a group of small objects somewhere beyond Neptune and Pluto. Perhaps they were made up of leftover material from when the planets first formed. Kuiper believed some

The Kuiper Belt was named for Gerard Kuiper, an astronomer who believed comets came from beyond Pluto.

Comets are chunks
of ice and rock that
orbit in space.

comets, which are chunks of ice and rock, may come from here. But Kuiper didn't find any of these objects during his lifetime. So most other astronomers forgot his idea.

Then in 1992, astronomers Jane Luu and David Jewitt found a small, icy object far beyond Pluto. In 1993, they found another one. Since then, many more of these small objects have been found in a belt, or area, that circles in the outer solar system.

People search the sky to discover new stars and planets.

The objects range in size from 62 to 248 miles (100 to 400 km) across. Astronomers say these objects are a lot like Pluto and Charon. Some even call them "Plutinos," which means little Plutos. They think there may be thousands of these objects orbiting in what is now called the "Kuiper Belt." They also believe this is where one kind of comet is formed.

Is Pluto a Planet?

Pluto has been a puzzle ever since Clyde W. Tombaugh found it in 1930. It is different from all the other planets. Its size is small for a planet. In fact, seven moons in the solar system are bigger than Pluto!

Its location in the solar system is also a puzzle. The

Above is the sky as Tombaugh saw it in 1930. The arrow points to the new planet he discovered—Pluto.

planets closest to the Sun—
Mercury, Venus, Earth, and
Mars—are all "rocky" planets.
They have solid, rocky surfaces.

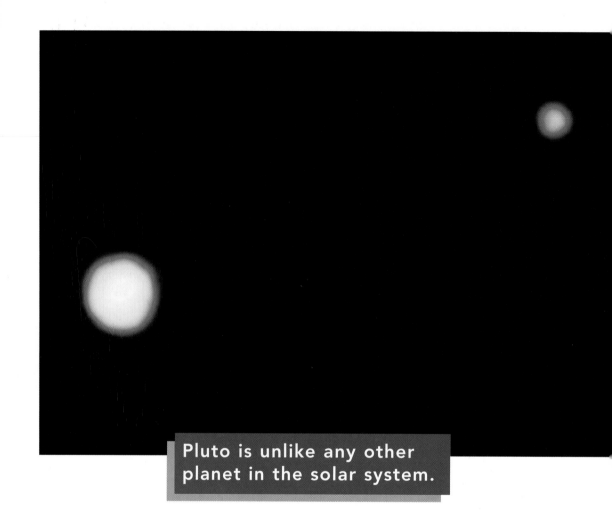

Pluto is unlike any other planet in the solar system.

The next four planets are the gas giants—Jupiter, Saturn, Uranus, and Neptune. But

Pluto is neither a rocky planet nor a gas giant.

The astronomers who think Pluto is not a planet say it is too small to be a planet. They say that Pluto and Charon are simply the largest of the icy objects in the Kuiper Belt. Other astronomers do not agree.

The International Astronomical Union (IAU) is the only organization that can name and label objects in space. For now, the IAU says Pluto is a planet.

Perhaps this will change when we learn more about it. A probe is scheduled to fly by Pluto and Charon sometime around 2012. The *Pluto-Kuiper Express* may be able to tell us if Pluto really is a planet.

One thing is certain. The solar system is a wonderful puzzle with many different pieces. Our thoughts about it will continue to change. We will always be finding new pieces to the puzzle.

The *Pluto-Kuiper Express* will reveal many secrets of the planet.

41

Pluto Quick Facts

Diameter	1,412 miles (2,272 km)
Average distance from the Sun	3.7 billion miles (5.9 billion km)
Average temperature	−378° to −396° F (−228° to −238° C)
Rotation	6 Earth-days, plus 9 hours
Length of year	248 Earth-years
Moons	1

Missions to Pluto

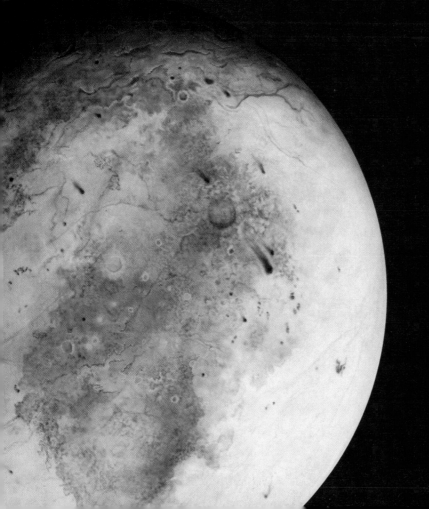

Mission	Launch Date
Pluto-Kuiper Express (USA)	Planned for 2003 or 2004

To Find Out More

Here are more places to learn about Pluto and other planets in space:

 **Books**

Asimov, Isaac. **A Double Planet?: Pluto and Charon.** Gareth Stevens, 1996.

Bailey, Donna. **The Far Planets.** Steck-Vaughn Company, 1991.

Brewer, Duncan. **The Outer Planets: Uranus, Neptune, Pluto.** Marshall Cavendish, 1993.

Cole, Joanna. **The Magic School Bus: Lost in the Solar System.** Scholastic, Inc., 1990.

Wetterer, Margaret K. **Clyde Tombaugh and the Search for Planet X.** Carolrhoda Books, 1996.

Organizations and Online Sites

The Children's Museum of Indianapolis

3000 N. Meridian Street
Indianapolis, IN 46208-4716
(317) 924-5431
http://childrensmuseum.org/sq1.htm

Visit the SpaceQuest Planetarium to see what it has to offer, including a view of this month's night sky.

National Aeronautics and Space Administration (NASA)

http://www.nasa.gov

At NASA's home page, you can access information about its exciting history and present resources and missions.

National Air and Space Museum

Smithsonian Institution
601 Independence Ave. SW
Washington, DC 20560
(202) 357-1300
http://www.nasm.si.edu/

The National Air and Space Museum site gives you up-to-date information about its programs and exhibits.

The Nine Planets

http://seds.lpl.arizona.edu/nineplanets/nineplanets/

Take a multimedia tour of the solar system and all its planets and moons.

Space Telescope Science Institute

3700 San Martin Drive
Johns Hopkins University
Homewood Campus
Baltimore, MD 21218
(410) 338-4700
http://www.stsci.edu//

The Space Telescope Science Institute operates the Hubble Space Telescope. Visit this site to see pictures of the telescope's outer-space view.

Windows to the Universe

http://windows.engin.umich.edu/

This site lets you click on all nine planets to find information about each one. It also covers many other space subjects, including important historical figures, scientists, and astronauts.

Important Words

astronomer a scientist who studies objects in space

atmosphere the gases surrounding a planet

axis an imaginary line about which a planet turns

comet a ball of frozen water, gases, and dust that orbits the Sun

gravity the force that pulls objects toward a planet's center

orbit to travel around an object

pole either end of a planet's axis

probe a spacecraft used to study space

rotate to spin

telescope an instrument that makes faraway objects look closer

Index

Meet the Author

Larry Dane Brimner is a former teacher and author of more than fifty books for children. His most recent titles for Children's Press are the Rookie Readers *How Many Ants?*, *Dinosaurs Dance*, and *Lightning Liz*. His True Book titles include *The World Wide Web*, *E-Mail*, and *Skiing*. He lives with his chow-chow Buddy in California and Colorado.